Pomalo: the Croatian Secret to Happy

Eat, sleep, celebrate to a healthy mind & body

Mary Ann Skaro

Dalmatian Media

Copyright © 2023 by Mary Ann Skaro

All rights reserved.

No part of this book may be reproduced in any form or by any electronic or mechanical means, including information storage and retrieval systems, without written permission from the author, except for the use of brief quotations in a book review.

I would like to dedicate this book to my Family. It was a team effort. My husband for supporting my dream. Ana for her creativity and illustration. Luka for his technical and design skills. Finally, Anthony for constantly motivating us straight to the finish line.

Contents

1. You Want The Truth — Can You Handle The Truth?   1
2. After the Rain — Rainbows   5
3. C'mon Let's Do the Hustle Culture   7
4. Burn Baby Burn-Out   9
5. Hurry Up and Slow Down   13
6. Wine a Little — Laugh a Lot   17
7. An Ounce of Pomalo is a Pound of Cure   21
8. The 7 Principles of Pomalo   23
9. Can We Fix It? Yes We Can   41

    About the Author   45

Chapter 1

You Want The Truth – Can You Handle The Truth?

You may wake up one morning, look in the mirror as you get ready for the day, and not recognize yourself. After all, it's not hard to lose yourself in this fast-paced world. Everyone has their problems. But, the pace and manner in which we live our lives has sprouted roots of ever bigger challenges.

For some, it happens gradually and silently. Others experience a cataclysmic event that shakes them to their very core. For me, it was a little of both.

The trick is to recognize it and accept this unpopular truth: that our evolved modern day mode of life is damaging to us. It is the antithesis of happiness. If you're brave and willing to shake things up a bit, be prepared to think outside the box and consider some ideas that border on conspiracy theory. Read on because you might just change your life for the better. At the very least, you'll go on the vacation of a lifetime…

I recall putting off returning several pieces of clothing I had purchased for my kids; I was too busy with other things. The bag of clothes had been sitting on my bedroom chair for weeks. When I finally made it into the store, the clerk informed me I went beyond the thirty-day return policy. I was denied a refund but was graciously granted a store credit instead. I recall my palms starting to sweat, my heart pounding, and this anger bubbling inside my chest. In a curt voice, I demanded a full refund; I explained to the manager I did not want a store credit to a retailer that did not honor the customer. I dug my heels in and would not budge on my stance.

The manager, bless her heart, was so patient with me, and in that brief moment her kindness knocked me into awareness. I remember stepping back and becoming an observer of my amplified emotions. Seconds felt like minutes as I took several deep breaths and began processing everything. It was as if I was resetting my mind and senses.

I walked out of the store feeling embarrassed, and empty. What had just happened? What had I become? I began to realize that life for me was no longer about the journey and experiences. Instead, it was solely about the destination — success. I was spending my days racing against the clock to check off the boxes of my increasingly ambitious 'To Do' lists. All the while losing sight of who I was, and what I enjoyed.

You Want The Truth – Can You Handle The Truth?

Life was becoming mechanical and efficient, completely bereft of personality. I was at a crossroads. I remember asking myself whether this brand of "success" really made me happy. The answer was a resounding NO!

Chapter 2

After the Rain – Rainbows

I've been fortunate to spend time in many beautiful and inspiring places both near and far. There is no doubt being on vacation is nurturing and exudes a sense of calm irrespective of the destination. But, despite my Croatian heritage, only after several trips there had it become apparent that Croatia offered something special. There were important life lessons to learn from the people, their culture, and its geography. Something intangible that evaded me for so many years.

I recall vividly exiting the plane, descending the stairs, and arriving on the tarmac; there's no sky bridge at the airport in Zagreb. There was something in the air — an energy that was both rejuvenating and tranquil. But I couldn't fully appreciate what was happening around me. As we were leaving the airport my brother-in-law ushered us to an outdoor cafe, "Let's have a coffee," he said, so casually. I remember thinking, "Why are we sitting down? Why don't we just take it to go?" This was to be my first clue and a stark contrast to the hurry and hustle culture I had become accustomed to living in Chicago.

As we were making our way into the city I noticed gas stations; as small as they were, they had sun umbrellas and chairs for customers to relax and enjoy a coffee like a pop-up café. Something told me this was more than simply a marketing ploy to attract more business. Instead, the scene immediately signaled the essence of slowing down. That was my second clue.

Despite this, my instinctual nature to multi-task was going full tilt. On vacation I was writing an email, while trying to explain to my taxi driver how long and far my husband's commute was to and from the hospital where he worked. He joked that "to Europeans 100 years is a short time but 100 kilometers is a long distance; but to Americans, 100 years is a long time and 100 kilometers is a short distance." That was my third clue, but I was still bewildered.

I found it funny that a Croatian taxi driver suggested we spend too much time in a car. I remarked there was a lot to get done and only so many hours in the day. He laughed wryly and said, "Americans need to remember: there's always tomorrow."

And then he uttered a single word: Pomalo.

The mystery was revealed. Everything was now in focus. This was my very first touchpoint to the unassuming allure of Pomalo culture.

Chapter 3

C'mon Let's Do the Hustle Culture

Had I been so blinded by ambition or was I just trying to keep up with the Joneses? How could I have been so numb while I was racing through life? Success, growing wealth, and extravagant experiences notwithstanding.

Indeed, many, past and present, have flocked to the 'New World' in search of opportunity and the promise of the American dream. However, this was a difficult path filled with risk and hardship. Pardon the pun, but fast forward a few hundred years and this 'American Dream' has become a veritable nightmare. The thirst for success has metamorphosed into the present day grind that is Hustle Culture.

Hustle Culture sucks you in like a vortex and holds you hostage to your dreams of obtaining a beautiful house in the suburbs, nice cars, and luxurious vacations. Increasing materialism has become the justification for pouring your whole life into work. This addictive behavior was normalized because the commerce that ensued was profitable, good for the economy, and the result of admirable hard work and productivity. Certainly, corporations and governments, who gained the most, further propagated Hustle Culture with an unprecedented marketing campaign. It didn't help that personal electronic devices like the iPhone were released making workers accessible at all times. Under the guise of progress and promising productivity the development of social media and associated advertising on these platforms only intensified Hustle Culture and materialism.

The lines between work and home were officially blurred. Soon we began to see 'Hustle' printed on t-shirts, mugs, and tote bags. Big corporations were also pushing this narrative: Nike launched an ad called 'Rise and Grind'. Multi-millionaire influencers like Gary Vaynerchuk emerged spreading Hustle Culture as a way of life with the motto, "Wake up before everybody else and work into the night."

Similarly, governments struggling to fund public programs have increasingly demanded productivity and efficiency from their workforces. For example, publicly-funded health care workers who experienced unprecedented burnout fresh off the heels of the pandemic are forced to consider performance metrics, academic deliverables, and accountability.

How can you be expected to save lives if you cannot save yourself?

Chapter 4

Burn Baby Burn-Out

Hustle culture puts work at the center of life. Long working hours are praised and glorified. Time off is seen as laziness. If you are not hustling, you are failing.

Consequently, a success-at-all-costs attitude prevails. You might be wondering — costs? And then it strikes you: "Wait — there are negative consequences?"

The establishment rewards you for your productivity. We like rewards and the dopamine that is released in our brains. Soon it becomes like an addiction where instant gratification supplants all else. Moreover, the narrative that is spun is that any negative consequences of the Hustle Culture mindset are merely "the price of success". But you may already sense the invisible wounds that have been imprinted on your soul, the psychological damage, and physical toll.

Hustle Culture has led to 'Hurry Sickness'. Rushing is a form of stress; it is the stress of having too many things to do and not enough time. If we only had a dollar every time we heard that. Now buckle up for a little science.

The body's stress response is similar whether the stressor is physical, psychological, or emotional. When we are placed in a stressful situation, our brains trigger the release of cortisol and adrenaline from the adrenal glands. This activates the sympathetic nervous system. In this alarm stage the body assembles its defenses to prepare for fight-or-flight, to protect against imminent danger. Simultaneously, the off signal is sent to non-essential systems that are not immediately needed for survival. This includes digestion, growth, reproduction, and immunity to name a few. So you might experience nausea, indigestion, and heartburn as emptying of the stomach is delayed. Similarly, it also explains an enhanced susceptibility to infections like the common cold due to stress.

Normally, stressors come and go and our bodies enter a state of repair allowing for recovery from injury. However, in the Hustle Culture lifestyle the rush is constant, and the stress is sustained. Persistent excess cortisol and adrenaline then have more damaging consequences, mentally and physically. The mind and body enter an exhaustion phase that leads to anxiety, depression, decreased social life, and insomnia.

Just in case that hasn't gotten your attention, cortisol causes obesity, loose and fragile skin, increases oil production leading to acne, promotes hair loss and premature graying. In essence, the Hustle Culture accelerates aging and it can rob you of your beauty.

But with a healthy dose of sarcasm, I wouldn't dream of suggesting the society we live in is vain. Instead of changing to a healthier mindset many choose the quick fix like breast augmentation, and Botox or filler injections. As if beauty and self-worth are found at the edge of a scalpel or bottom of a bottle.

Now I have your attention: the good news is that with awareness of the evils of Hustle Culture we can make changes.

However, change is hard, particularly when people don't know why there is a need to change or that there is even a problem in the first place. You can usually trace resistance to change back to a lack of awareness. It's not as if burnout shows up at your door and announces itself with a formal introduction.

"Hello there. My name is Burnout and I'm going to ruin your life!"

It is a stealthy intruder that makes itself at home in your body and grows quietly. Soon your days become mundane and fly by. You are exhausted yet gas-lighted by nothing at all. A sudden explosion of emotions is triggered by a situation that does not warrant a dramatic response.

Does this sound familiar?

Chapter 5

Hurry Up and Slow Down

Self-awareness is the first step towards slowing down. Just by a change of mindset, take a pause, notice your surroundings, and experience with all of the senses, you become grounded in the moment. This seemingly small change in the perception of our surroundings can shift towards activation of the parasympathetic nervous system and initiate a state of natural restoration.

Remember the stress response is initiated in the brain and so we can actually control our physiology just by changing our perception of the world around us.

We all know people who find battles all around them. They find a crusade in everything from school, relationships, politics, economics — you name it. It's not that these things are unimportant or you shouldn't stand up for what you believe in. However, we can take things too far and it can begin to consume us. You don't want to be that person because now you know the consequences and where that leads. It will compromise health and jeopardize relationships important to emotional wellbeing.

When you slow down and soften your view of the world you become at rest. It's in this relaxed state that your body becomes calm, your heart rate drops, and your metabolic and gastrointestinal systems function normally. Interestingly, metabolism of your food is more favorable, weight is moderated, and immunity, sexual function, and energy are all heightened.

However, we literally need to be shaken out of this amnestic state and thrust back into reality to appreciate just how pervasive life in the Hustle is. It's like life is happening and not actually being lived. It's like we are all plugged into the Matrix. Choose the red pill and choose to live the Pomalo lifestyle, and there is no looking back — I assure you.

You are here because you are ready to nip your hustle culture in the bud.

It's not that being productive is bad, but working your body to over-exhaustion is. The pressure to constantly work harder and faster is suffocating. Working this hard isn't your dream. Your work is being harnessed towards corporate greed. Governments are complicit, misleading you to believe they are interested in your wellbeing.

My story isn't a conspiracy theory, but a cautionary tale and warning to re-evaluate your life before it's too late.

I set a match to a glorified hustle culture life and watched it burn down. As it burned, I felt my soul rising out like a phoenix ready to live differently, intentionally, and on my own terms.

Luckily, my Croatian heritage and frequent visits there were a shining example of the way life could be lived. After all, human life is a precious gift to be cherished, and not consumed like another log on the fire of progress.

Chapter 6

Wine a Little – Laugh a Lot

In what follows I will share a few anecdotes, tips, tricks, and hacks of Pomalo in the hope I can show you a more peaceful and fulfilling life path. Who knows — you may take a trip to Croatia and experience the magic first hand.

But first let me point out the definition of the word Pomalo which, in Croatian, means:

Slow down. Take it easy. Don't stress. Relax.

This definition barely scratches the surface of the true meaning.

Its origins are from the western coast of Croatia in a region called Dalmacija. The very same region which gave its name to the loyal and lovable white and black spotted dog. The

Dalmatian has graced many firehouses and Disney films over the years.

To the people of Dalmacija, Pomalo is not merely a word, but a way of life. Affectionately, it is "how [they] do things". It is this laid-back approach to life that has often put Dalmatians at the center of a "vic", or joke, in Croatian. Seemingly, imitation is the sincerest form of flattery as other Croatians instinctually spend the entire month of August on the Adriatic coast.

Let's lightheartedly examine the Ten Commandments of the Dalmatian:

1. Man is born tired and lives to rest.
2. Love your bed as you do yourself.
3. Rest during the day so you can sleep at night.
4. Don't work, work kills.
5. When you see someone resting, help them.
6. Don't do today what you can do tomorrow.
7. Do less than you can, and what you can, pass on to someone else.
8. There is salvation in the shade, no-one dies from resting.
9. Work brings illness, don't die young.
10. When you have the desire to work, sit down and it'll pass.

Reading these commandments you might think that Dalmatians are lazy. In fact, it's the contrary: they are extremely hard workers completing many of their tasks early in the morning, likely before most of us even start our day. The fishermen return at daylight with their catch ready for the market. Farmers plowed and sowed their fields by hand only with the help of a donkey.

It reminds me of another "vic" my husband's grandfather told him as a child. To paraphrase, a Russian brags to a Dalmatian that they were the first to put a dog on the moon. The Dalmatian, unimpressed, replies, "Meni je tovar svaki dan na suncu," which means, "My donkey is [on] the sun every day."

The fruits of the Dalmatians' labors were evident in the markets daily, feeding the people of the region and tourists alike. But, there was a time and a place for work, and many more times to savor life and its many experiences.

Chapter 7

An Ounce of Pomalo is a Pound of Cure

From where you are standing I'm sure the cure for your Hustle Culture seems like a daunting task. The daily grind has been drilled deeply into our psyche. It is heavily entrenched and not easily uprooted.

But seeing Pomalo in action, its simplicity, and realizing what life should and could be will quickly win you over. Dalmatians have handed down this way of life for generations, having 'worked hard' to perfect the easygoing mindset that is Pomalo. In fact, the seven basic principles of Pomalo are fun and easy. They are both intuitive and entertaining. I'm sure that once you have read about them, you will want to visit Croatia, whether you take a trip to the Dalmatian coast or not. These Pomalo practices teach you to slow down, savor life, and celebrate your way to a healthy mind and body.

Chapter 8

The 7 Principles of Pomalo

1. Mind Over Matter – Of Time

In North America, the 'time is money' mentality sees everyone rushing from one task to the next. Every day and night is filled to excess.

But, you can always make more money. You can't make more time.

Then why is it that westerners squander this rare and precious resource? There is no savoring of the experiences that span this time. It flies by at the speed of light in a blur. There is a brief surge of dopamine in the brain associated with instant gratification. Meaningful memory, however, cannot form under these circumstances nor can durable satisfaction. Instead, resentment over lost time and burnout ensue.

The Pomalo lifestyle is the antidote for this toxin. Realizing that time is our most valuable commodity, the Dalmatian slows down time. Believe it or not, Pomalo is the Croatian time-travel machine. This shouldn't come as a surprise: Croatia is the country of origin of brilliant inventors such as Nikola Tesla and more recently Mate Rimac, known for creating the world's fastest production electric vehicle. Why couldn't a Dalmatian develop a time-travel machine?

All joking aside, another way of looking at the act of slowing down is the intention of making the most of every moment. Relationships, experiences, sensations are all composed of moments in time. The effortless extraction of the best of these is a treasured skill of Croatians.

Another way of conveying this is how Croatians value quality over quantity. For instance, Croatians take great pride in their winemaking. Miljenko Grgić put Napa Valley on the map of winemaking after his Chardonnay beat the French in 1976. Later, he proved the Zinfandel grape has origins in the Croatian Plavac Mali variety. Yet, Croatian wine production will never reach the top of Europe or the world. Nor is it ever intended to do so. Instead, the focus of Croatian winemaking prioritizes quality over quantity. To Croatians, it's not about increasing production or maximizing profits; pride in the product and the process is meant to be shared and savored with friends and family.

Many of the Croatian diaspora continue the tradition of winemaking no matter where they live. It becomes a point of conversation and a story or expression of love conveyed by the artisan. My own father, well into his eighties, continues to make his wine, and we have spent many memorable occasions around the table drinking it.

2. It's Not All About Money: Nije u šoldima sve

In a popular Croatian folk song, a father passionately describes the unrivaled beauty and serenity of life in Dalmacija. He implores his son to stay at his side and warns him there is more to life than money. The song emphasizes the love of a father for his son and the importance of family. But, it also tells a story of the romance between a man and his birthplace. It teaches us that Dalmacija is like a nurturing mother. The vistas feed our souls much like the fruits of the land and sea nourish us.

Sure, we need money to live and survive. But life in the western world has become a life of gluttony. A never-ending conveyor belt that prioritizes the accumulation of material wealth. But, with more come more and bigger problems. Case in point: that bigger home you aspire to garners greater taxes and mortgage, requiring a promotion and higher salary — translating into more responsibility and stress, with less free time to spend with family and friends, doing the things we love.

The father warns his son of the dangers of excess. He reminds him to slow down and savor every moment of the wonders of Dalmacija. It is a place, a people, and a way of life that has withstood foreign invaders. Those who sought to conquer have failed. Those who sought to shift the culture have themselves been won over or have given up trying. No more is this evident than in the following folk tale:

A Dalmatian sat on the shore every day looking out on the sea. An American tourist watched him every day doing nothing. Finally, the American couldn't stand it. So he approached the Dalmatian and asked, "Listen, why are you doing nothing all day, every day? You could buy nylon thread, and a hook. Throw it into the sea, catch a fish, sell the fish, and make money."

"And what then?" asked the Dalmatian.

"Then you buy more nylon, more hooks, catch more fish, sell them, and make more money!"

"And what then?" said the Dalmatian.

"And then you buy a boat, you go further from the coast where there are bigger fish. You catch bigger fish, you sell them, and make a lot of money!"

"And what then?" asked the Dalmatian.

The American was already annoyed, and said: "Well, then you have a lot of money. Buy a bigger boat and hire people. They catch a lot of big fish, sell them, make a lot of money, and you just sit back and enjoy!"

The Dalmatian calmly replied, "I'm already doing that."

3. To What Do I Owe the 'Simple' Pleasure? Gušt

Life has become increasingly complicated. Complexity can detract from life's simple pleasures. Hustle Culture has even popularized the concept of guilt when it comes to pleasures, as if there's something wrong with deriving joy from life — except for the American tenet of joy in a hard day's work.

Instead, Dalmatians have become experts at enjoying the simple things in life. So much so that they have a word for it: gušt (pronounced Gu-sht) is a slang word used by the people of Dalmacija, which means 'simple pleasures'. Common examples include a barbeque with friends, lying on the beach, enjoying a coffee, or fishing.

However, if you observe them closely, you see a Dalmatian can find joy in almost anything, be it by simply watching the waves crash onto the shore, or experiencing the scent of lavender and pine while taking a leisurely stroll on a promenade. It is as much a state of mind that is immune to boredom as it is the avoidance of extremes of happiness or sadness. Gušt becomes a lesson in life emphasizing the difference between necessity and the unnecessary. This existence strikes a harmony with its surroundings. It is fulfilling to resist the insatiable thirst for more that afflicts many westerners.

Consider the principle of gušt as your invitation to examine the world around you. To find joy in everything and everyone.

To start cultivating your own forms of gušt, you must first slow down. You can't be connected to the life force if you're too hurried to observe your surroundings. If you constantly feel pressure to perform, life's simple pleasures will certainly be obscured from your view.

You might think you already enjoy many things in life. Americans call these things hobbies and they could include reading, travel, sports, gastronomy, and so on. But this is not gušt. At least, not until you close your eyes and apply the same mindset you experience while you watch that Sunday afternoon football game to something mundane.

Gušt is sitting on your porch watching the rain fall on your field, feeling the satisfaction that it is helping your fruit trees to flourish. An American analogy would be enjoying a beautiful landscape while commuting to work in the morning. Commuting is notoriously a stressful activity that many dread, but the ability to extract joy from even this chore is a stunning example of gušt.

Pomalo is not a destination you travel to; rather it's a journey to a state of mind you are always in. Pleasure gets you in touch with the here and now, allowing your mind to indulge in the joy of the moment. Gušt is about savoring and valuing pleasure. It's about strengthening our health and relationships with self and others. Creating more gušt in your day requires you to examine your calendar and see where you can fit in more moments of pause — and set up blocks of time when you are not available for anyone else, whether it's to take a walk, take a nap, or just sit still.

Feel free to hang up a sign that reads "Gone Fishing". You are celebrating and honoring your time for joy. North Americans have branded this activity as 'mindfulness'; the Dalmatian need not pay any mind. It is instinctual and has been in practice there for generations. There is no need for chants, scents, psychotropics, mantras, or any adjunct whatsoever. It isn't something coerced or forced. Perhaps that is its allure.

4. Eat, Drink: Ćakula

The idiom 'eat, drink, and be merry', particularly the social aspect of dining, is important to Croatians. The art of conversation, which is often a light topic bordering on gossip, is known as ćakula (pronounced cha-ku-la). It is the focal point of sharing a meal, dessert, or just an espresso.

Think about this for a moment. When you engage in conversation with a friend or acquaintance, it is an opportunity to tell them what's happening in your day. Maybe vent about problems. Share your hopes and dreams. Conversation is a two-way street and so listening to your companion is also a big part of ćakula. Together, you make a community of support for one another. This is like your own version of therapy minus punching in a time clock and paying at the end of your session. Consequently, there are several physical, psychological, and emotional benefits. In short, connecting over a meal relieves stress and places you in a restful state, allowing the mind and body to repair. For this reason, you won't see a Dalmatian eating or drinking alone. Nor is there any rush.

Do you see now why the concept of a 'coffee to go' or 'fast food' is completely foreign? It's not uncommon to engage in ćakula for hours over a coffee.

Placing the obvious benefits of companionship aside for a moment, recall that the stress response characteristic of Hustle Culture shuts off the digestive system and alters metabolism unfavorably. If you often eat on the run or under stress, you will gain weight despite avoiding overeating and consuming a balanced and healthy diet. So it is just as much about how you eat as it is about what you are eating. Not to mention that it's difficult to enjoy your meal if you are rushing through it.

When you take a trip to Croatia you are going to experience some of the most delicious foods. Take the time to savor every bite. After all, I guarantee it was prepared meticulously with love using the old ways. No cutting corners. Dishes are prepared the way Baba/Baka (which means grandmother in Croatian) used to make it. I have been surprised to see Baba (Dalmacija) in the kitchen when I've asked to meet the chef.

As you might have guessed, food and drink are an important part of Croatian culture. Given the history of the region there are many influences that have shaped the cuisine. Food of the interior has been influenced by neighboring Austrian, Hungarian, and Turkish fare. Whereas coastal areas such as Dalmacija feature Mediterranean ingredients including olive oil, citrus, and herbs. Croatian gastronomy is among the best in Europe, much to the delight of the many tourists who visit every year.

Croatia has an ideal climate and conditions for diverse farming. Policies deter the use of genetically modified organisms, preservatives, and pesticides. A farm- and/or sea-to-table approach provides an unforgettable dining experience. Portion control, once again maintaining focus on quality over quantity, leaves patrons satisfied.

Not that what you are eating isn't important, but Croatians put extra focus on who they dine with and the manner in which they consume food and drink is a priority.

The Pomalo lifestyle is about eating "in season foods" including fruits, vegetables, and proteins. Think about foods that will nourish and energize your body, rather than foods that make you feel bloated and sluggish.

In most cases this means limiting your intake of processed foods filled with preservatives. These are banned. When you buy a loaf of bread at the pekara or bakery you notice it's stale the next day. There are no preservatives. Even after eating the signature Burek, a savory strudel of meat or cheese, you'll feel light as a feather.

I remember when my daughter first saw a watermelon in Split. She asked me what those black things inside the melon were. I grew up in the Eighties when watermelons looked like they do in Croatia today: they have seeds. I stopped and thought about her question, and realized I only purchased seedless watermelons for my family. They had no idea what a real watermelon is supposed to look like.

You will find high-quality foods like the best olive oil, truffles, and tuna tartare you've ever tasted. Croatians are known for creating and consuming some of the best foods with locally sourced ingredients. Regular trips to the market to buy in-season fruits and vegetables is a daily task. Meal preparation is fresh and on demand. It is an artisanal experience that locals take pride in.

Local markets across Croatia are usually simple but can be elaborate. It's where the locals haggle and buy most of their food. I pulled out my haggling tricks and took to one of the stands in Split where a lovely woman named Ljubica was selling oranges and lemons. In Croatian, I told Ljubica I wanted four oranges and one lemon; she gave me a price of forty kuna and I negotiated it down to thirty-five. I was proud as a peacock — until she threw in an extra lemon and said for the whole thing 40 kuna. I agreed to the price despite not needing the extra lemon. I felt I was getting a bargain… or was I? Ljubica had this smile from ear to ear. She wished me well, and I was off to the next stand of fresh produce to continue my haggling.

It's all seasonal. One week I saw piles of apricots. The following week it was peaches until their peak was over. Croatians only eat fruit when they are in season because that's when they taste the best. You won't get strawberries in December. But guess what? You wouldn't want them. We have become so accustomed in North America to having fruits all year round. You must have tasted raspberries in January that have traveled thousands of miles and they just don't taste the same as fresh, in season, locally sourced produce.

This seasonality helps to maintain the pristine Croatian environment. Tourism is its primary export. Local farmers are cheerful, take pride in their products, and supporting them is good for your soul and your wallet.

5. Enjoy Life – Look the Part: Uživaj

Uživaj means to enjoy.

Your clothes, style, and appearance are an outward expression of what you are feeling. Hopefully, after implementing the Pomalo principles, you are ready to enjoy/uživaj your life with style. This may sound superficial, but hear me out.

Your personal style can shape how you show up every day. Clothes have a way of making us feel confident and happy so dressing in clothes that exude positive emotions is a wonderful way to start our days and project a positive attitude.

Your opinion of yourself is important, and one way to embody a positive self image is through your clothing. It doesn't necessarily mean you must wear expensive attire; instead, take the time to ensure you are well groomed and neatly dressed. To Croatians, there is no such thing as being overdressed. Every moment you are out in public is an opportunity to make a positive impression. This is most evident when sipping a coffee at a café, attending mass at church, picking up a few things at the market, and most certainly when you're out on the town at a nightclub.

I decided to test this theory out for myself. Thinking carefully about every piece of clothing, I reached for a beautiful dress, added some earrings, a touch of makeup, and shoes that looked and felt great for strolling. I resisted my nature to quickly throw on clothes and instead slowed down to thoroughly consider every detail. After all, no one is going to have a higher opinion of you than you. And you are worth it.

I realized in that moment every time I slow down and make an effort to dress well, I am subconsciously reminding myself I matter. It distills down to loving yourself. Slowing down to plan outfits that make me feel fabulous feels so pleasurable.

As I stepped out on the streets of Split that day, I noticed myself smile and exude a level of joy and a sparkle. If you pay attention to the locals, you will see they are all dressed stylishly and neatly for a coffee with a friend or a trip to the market. They make an effort to bring beauty and positivity to every interaction, even those with strangers. There is an air of elegance and grace emanating from the streets of Zagreb and Split that seemed different from what I was used to on Michigan Avenue in Chicago which is arguably one of the most opulent streets in the US.

This Croatian style is not pretentious; rather it's just a way of being and enjoying a few dressier pieces in your wardrobe, and is yet another example of prioritizing quality over quantity. Instead of buying clothes that are a bargain, consider buying one beautiful piece of clothing per shopping excursion for a more stylish and sustainable wardrobe. Although I must say that nowadays you really can dress chic on almost any budget.

Take the time and make the effort to avoid rolling out of bed in a hoodie and tights to make a trip to the grocery store. You will see how wonderful looking your best all the time makes you feel.

6. Move for Life: Kolo

Pomalo living is setting aside time for movement. As much as Pomalo is about slowing down to experience joy, Croatians have a very physical culture because they value time away from the grind of work. Engaging in physical activity is critical for their mental health and happiness.

Now this does not mean you become a professional athlete; it's about giving yourself permission to unwind with sport or another physical activity like dancing. In the west, people move to moderate weight and maintain health. This is called exercise.

Croatians have a passion for movement. It isn't a chore. Hence, the population is generally slim, and vibrant. Movement is an expression of culture and heritage, a social infrastructure, and a form of national identity.

Croatia is much like a confederation of regions dating back more than a thousand years. Each region has distinctive dialects, ceremonial dress, and folk music and dance called Kolo. Interestingly, Kolo was a form of entertainment and the basis of celebrations. It was an opportunity for socializing and even became an expression of courtship. The song and dance even in wedding celebrations can last days spanning multiple villages or locations.

Croatian folklore and Kolo are a tradition that is preserved to this day among diaspora around the world. Kolo constitutes one of the important modes of preserving the Croatian language and culture.

Croatians love to dance. Everything from traditional kolo to more modern forms of festivals are extremely popular. The word Kolo means circle, which includes groups of people holding hands and performing various dances. Kolo is usually accompanied with fast-paced instrumental music similar to the mandolin but called the tamburica. It is often simple and easy to learn choreographed dances and is a great way to meet people and get your heart rate up.

No fear if kolo sounds too intimidating. There are so many fun festivals that get people singing and dancing.

Music is known to stimulate pleasure and rewards areas like the orbitofrontal cortex, located directly behind the eyes. Music also activates the cerebellum at the base of the brain which is in charge of time and movement. There are so many opportunities to dance in Croatia. Plus dancing is a mental break from the rest of your day, and releases endorphins. Anyone who has danced all night at a wedding or a music festival like Ultra Europe in Split knows there is something about dancing that makes you feel great.

The most important expression of the Croatian identity is through sport. Have you ever wondered how Croatia, with a population under four million people, has produced some of the world's best athletes? Croatians are among the world's best in football, basketball, tennis, handball, and skiing — to name a few. The Croatia national football team has won bronze (1998) and silver (2018) medals at the World Cup. As I'm writing this they are making another fabled run for the world's most prestigious trophy. Go Vatreni!

Dalmatians, in particular, have an unwavering passion for their local football club Hajduk Split. In winning and losing, it is an undying love that is like a religion. It is an indispensable focus of conversation, a catalyst for social gathering, and a holy experience to attend a match. All of Dalmacija pauses for its matches in a collective expression of Pomalo.

If sport or dancing is not your thing, consider taking a walk in nature. Yes, even in cold climates it's refreshing to feel the cool brisk wind on your body. Connecting with nature is peaceful and relaxing.

7. And On the Seventh Day, Rest: Fjaka

In 670 AD Croatians embraced the Catholic faith, entering a sacred treaty with Pope St Agatho. God's protection from foreign invaders was bestowed upon the Croatian people. Later, Croatians were instrumental in preserving the Church through their heroic resistance to Tartaric and Ottoman invaders. Croatians are a very spiritual people. Even God, having created the Earth and everything on it rested on the seventh day. Hence, the act of resting holds a very sacred meaning among Croatians who believe we are created in His image.

Dalmatians have taken the concept of rest to a whole new level.

Again, many have mistaken this for laziness; instead, it is a state of bliss or zen achieved during relaxation in the sun. Not surprisingly there is a word for it: fjaka (pronounced fee-ya-kah). Fjaka often manifests as taking breaks throughout the day, preferably a nap. It is believed that the ensuing relaxed state of mind helps to cure or prevent illness, and makes you look and feel younger. To which I say, sign me up!

As I previously mentioned, it's in the rest state (parasympathetic activation) that your body and mind recover and repair. In fjaka you become calm, your heart rate drops, and thinking melts away. Dalmatians believe it's a God-given gift, as you turn off your thinking and simply rest. It is a way to recharge your batteries.

Not surprisingly, coming from the US to visit Croatia, I am always in a rush to do more. Some of the locals told me that I needed to fjaka more. At the time, I thought it was a rude and inappropriate comment. Admittedly, I mistook it for a certain four letter work. My sister sensed my misunderstanding and leaned over to say, "Mare, fjaka means to take a nap." Breathing a sigh of relief, I said, "In that case, why aren't more people doing it during the day?"

But they are doing it, and I was just too busy to notice.

Remember, you won't see the beauty and wonder around you if you don't take the time to notice. A short twenty-minute nap allows your body and mind to relax without entering deeper sleep. A short nap is good for your overall health, memory, and creativity. Ironically, this state of relaxation would most benefit people in Hustle Culture, but they may not be ready to fjaka around.

All joking aside, sometimes we need something provocative to shake us into awareness. It just so happens in this instance it's the opposite, more like a sheep in wolf's clothing.

Chapter 9

Can We Fix It? Yes We Can

These seven Pomalo principles are meant to teach you to slow down, savor life, and celebrate your way to a healthy body and mind. These practices are designed to guide you through a gallery of possibilities for greater happiness. Imagine what your life will be like when you embody the Pomalo lifestyle: you will look vibrant, feel vivacious, and walk into a room with renewed confidence. You can and you will create a Pomalo life because you are worth it. You'll have a newly reborn sense of self and wellbeing.

I understand some of these practices may feel unfamiliar at first. We all know change is hard. But, this is mission critical and our most precious resource — time is wasting. I encourage you to set aside your judgment. You have been brainwashed into sacrificing your mind, body, and soul in pursuit of someone else's greed. Do yourself a favor and become open to trying something new.

Integrating these simple steps of relaxation into your day and allowing your body to recharge will make you look and feel younger. By now you are too familiar with hustle culture and ready to kick that life to the curb. You know the symptoms and the warning signs of fatigue and displeasure. Don't ignore them and continue following all the other lemmings running off the edge of the cliff. Work is not the center of your world — you and your wellbeing are.

Here are some declarations I want to see you embody:

- I work hard and play harder. In Pomalo there can be room for both.
- I rest often and take occasional days off.
- I indulge in delicious seasonal foods that nourish my body.
- I enjoy food and drink with company that makes me feel amazing.
- I move for life, and life is all about movement.
- I invest in myself, in my clothes, and in my appearance.
- I celebrate elegance and grace at every age.
- I am kind to myself.
- I am aware of my negative self-talk.
- I don't push myself to the point of exhaustion.
- I know my boundaries and when to say NO.
- I take breaks from digital devices, social media, and focus on nurturing my spiritual health.

- I host parties to celebrate my health, goals, and milestones.
- I make a toast to my Pomalo life: Življeli/cheers!

When you begin to slow down and savor all the miracles in your life, you'll be ready for the next big step: cooking Croatian Cuisine just like Baka/Baba.

About the Author

Mary Ann Skaro has a Masters degree in Health and Politics. She has worked on both sides of the wellness industry as a healthcare executive and as a life coach. She is a busy mom of three. Her spouse is a transplant surgeon, and so she has recognized the negative consequences of Hustle Culture and is passionate about ridding the world of stress.

The Croatian language and culture were an important part of her upbringing. She visited Croatia and became fascinated with the way of life there, so she did the research, interviewed the people, and wrote the book. In it she aims to bring a smile and teaches you to slow down and savor life's special moments.

Take a trip to Dalmacija and welcome to Croatian Pomalo. It will be unforgettable.

 instagram.com/crolicious_cooking

www.ingramcontent.com/pod-product-compliance
Lightning Source LLC
Chambersburg PA
CBHW041153110526
44590CB00027B/4217